中华人民共和国专利法

（中英文对照）

知识产权出版社

全国百佳图书出版单位

—北京—

图书在版编目（CIP）数据

中华人民共和国专利法：中英文对照/第十三届全国人民代表大会常务委员会著. —北京：知识产权出版社，2024.3
ISBN 978 - 7 - 5130 - 9320 - 0

Ⅰ. ①中…　Ⅱ. ①第…　Ⅲ. ①专利权法—中国—汉、英　Ⅳ. ①D923.42

中国国家版本馆 CIP 数据核字（2024）第 046015 号

责任编辑：卢海鹰　王瑞璞　　　　　　责任校对：潘凤越
封面设计：杨杨工作室·张　冀　　　　责任印制：刘译文

中华人民共和国专利法（中英文对照）

出版发行：	知识产权出版社 有限责任公司	网　址：	http：//www. ipph. cn
社　址：	北京市海淀区气象路 50 号院	邮　编：	100081
责编电话：	010 - 82000860 转 8116	责编邮箱：	wangruipu@ cnipr. com
发行电话：	010 - 82000860 转 8101/8102	发行传真：	010 - 82000893/82005070/82000270
印　刷：	天津嘉恒印务有限公司	经　销：	新华书店、各大网上书店及相关专业书店
开　本：	880mm×1230mm　1/32	印　张：	2
版　次：	2024 年 3 月第 1 版	印　次：	2024 年 3 月第 1 次印刷
字　数：	50 千字	定　价：	20.00 元

ISBN 978 - 7 - 5130 - 9320 - 0

目　录

中华人民共和国主席令

第五十五号

　　《全国人民代表大会常务委员会关于修改〈中华人民共和国专利法〉的决定》已由中华人民共和国第十三届全国人民代表大会常务委员会第二十二次会议于 2020 年 10 月 17 日通过，现予公布，自 2021 年 6 月 1 日起施行。

中华人民共和国主席　习近平

2020 年 10 月 17 日

中华人民共和国专利法

（1984 年 3 月 12 日第六届全国人民代表大会常务委员会第四次会议通过　根据 1992 年 9 月 4 日第七届全国人民代表大会常务委员会第二十七次会议《关于修改〈中华人民共和国专利法〉的决定》第一次修正　根据 2000 年 8 月 25 日第九届全国人民代表大会常务委员会第十七次会议《关于修改〈中华人民共和国专利法〉的决定》第二次修正　根据 2008 年 12 月 27 日第十一届全国人民代表大会常务委员会第六次会议《关于修改〈中华人民共和国专利法〉的决定》第三次修正　根据 2020 年 10 月 17 日第十三届全国人民代表大会常务委员会第二十二次会议《关于修改〈中华人民共和国专利法〉的决定》第四次修正）

目　录

第一章 总 则

第一条 为了保护专利权人的合法权益，鼓励发明创造，推动发明创造的应用，提高创新能力，促进科学技术进步和经济社会发展，制定本法。

第二条 本法所称的发明创造是指发明、实用新型和外观设计。

发明，是指对产品、方法或者其改进所提出的新的技术方案。

实用新型，是指对产品的形状、构造或者其结合所提出的适于实用的新的技术方案。

外观设计，是指对产品的整体或者局部的形状、图案或者其结合以及色彩与形状、图案的结合所作出的富有美感并适于工业应用的新设计。

第三条 国务院专利行政部门负责管理全国的专利工作；统一受理和审查专利申请，依法授予专利权。

省、自治区、直辖市人民政府管理专利工作的部门负责本行政区域内的专利管理工作。

第四条 申请专利的发明创造涉及国家安全或者重大利益需要保密的，按照国家有关规定办理。

第五条 对违反法律、社会公德或者妨害公共利益的发明创造，不授予专利权。

对违反法律、行政法规的规定获取或者利用遗传资源，并依赖该遗传资源完成的发明创造，不授予专利权。

第六条 执行本单位的任务或者主要是利用本单位的物质技术条件所完成的发明创造为职务发明创造。职务发明创造申请专利的权利属于该单位，申请被批准后，该单位为专利权人。该单位可以依法处置其职务发明创造申请专利的权利和专利权，促进相关发明创造的实施和运用。

非职务发明创造，申请专利的权利属于发明人或者设计人；申请被批准后，该发明人或者设计人为专利权人。

利用本单位的物质技术条件所完成的发明创造，单位与发明人或者设计人订有合同，对申请专利的权利和专利权的归属作出约定的，从其约定。

第七条　对发明人或者设计人的非职务发明创造专利申请，任何单位或者个人不得压制。

第八条　两个以上单位或者个人合作完成的发明创造、一个单位或者个人接受其他单位或者个人委托所完成的发明创造，除另有协议的以外，申请专利的权利属于完成或者共同完成的单位或者个人；申请被批准后，申请的单位或者个人为专利权人。

第九条　同样的发明创造只能授予一项专利权。但是，同一申请人同日对同样的发明创造既申请实用新型专利又申请发明专利，先获得的实用新型专利权尚未终止，且申请人声明放弃该实用新型专利权的，可以授予发明专利权。

两个以上的申请人分别就同样的发明创造申请专利的，专利权授予最先申请的人。

第十条　专利申请权和专利权可以转让。

中国单位或者个人向外国人、外国企业或者外国其他组织转让专利申请权或者专利权的，应当依照有关法律、行政法规的规定办理手续。

转让专利申请权或者专利权的，当事人应当订立书面合同，并向国务院专利行政部门登记，由国务院专利行政部门予以公告。专利申请权或者专利权的转让自登记之日起生效。

第十一条　发明和实用新型专利权被授予后，除本法另有规定的以外，任何单位或者个人未经专利权人许可，都不得实施其专利，即不得为生产经营目的制造、使用、许诺销售、销售、进口其专利产品，或者使用其专利方法以及使用、许诺销售、销售、进口依照该专利方法直接获得的产品。

外观设计专利权被授予后，任何单位或者个人未经专利权人许可，都不得实施其专利，即不得为生产经营目的制造、许诺销售、销售、进口其外观设计专利产品。

第十二条　任何单位或者个人实施他人专利的，应当与专利权人订立实施许可合同，向专利权人支付专利使用费。被许可人无权允许合同规定以外的任何单位或者个人实施该专利。

第十三条　发明专利申请公布后，申请人可以要求实施其发明的单位或者个人支付适当的费用。

第十四条　专利申请权或者专利权的共有人对权利的行使有约定的，从其约定。没有约定的，共有人可以单独实施或者以普通许可方式许可他人实施该专利；许可他人实施该专利的，收取的使用费应当在共有人之间分配。

除前款规定的情形外，行使共有的专利申请权或者专利权应当取得全体共有人的同意。

第十五条　被授予专利权的单位应当对职务发明创造的发明人或者设计人给予奖励；发明创造专利实施后，根据其推广应用的范围和取得的经济效益，对发明人或者设计人给予合理的报酬。

国家鼓励被授予专利权的单位实行产权激励，采取股权、期权、分红等方式，使发明人或者设计人合理分享创新收益。

第十六条 发明人或者设计人有权在专利文件中写明自己是发明人或者设计人。

专利权人有权在其专利产品或者该产品的包装上标明专利标识。

第十七条 在中国没有经常居所或者营业所的外国人、外国企业或者外国其他组织在中国申请专利的，依照其所属国同中国签订的协议或者共同参加的国际条约，或者依照互惠原则，根据本法办理。

第十八条 在中国没有经常居所或者营业所的外国人、外国企业或者外国其他组织在中国申请专利和办理其他专利事务的，应当委托依法设立的专利代理机构办理。

中国单位或者个人在国内申请专利和办理其他专利事务的，可以委托依法设立的专利代理机构办理。

专利代理机构应当遵守法律、行政法规，按照被代理人的委托办理专利申请或者其他专利事务；对被代理人发明创造的内容，除专利申请已经公布或者公告的以外，负有保密责任。专利代理机构的具体管理办法由国务院规定。

第十九条 任何单位或者个人将在中国完成的发明或者实用新型向外国申请专利的，应当事先报经国务院专利行政部门进行保密审查。保密审查的程序、期限等按照国务院的规定执行。

中国单位或者个人可以根据中华人民共和国参加的有关国际条约提出专利国际申请。申请人提出专利国际申请的，应当遵守前款规定。

国务院专利行政部门依照中华人民共和国参加的有关国际条约、本法和国务院有关规定处理专利国际申请。

对违反本条第一款规定向外国申请专利的发明或者实用新型，在中国申请专利的，不授予专利权。

第二十条 申请专利和行使专利权应当遵循诚实信用原则。不得滥用专利权损害公共利益或者他人合法权益。

滥用专利权，排除或者限制竞争，构成垄断行为的，依照《中华人民共和国反垄断法》处理。

第二十一条 国务院专利行政部门应当按照客观、公正、准确、及时的要求，依法处理有关专利的申请和请求。

国务院专利行政部门应当加强专利信息公共服务体系建设，完整、准确、及时发布专利信息，提供专利基础数据，定期出版专利公报，促进专利信息传播与利用。

在专利申请公布或者公告前，国务院专利行政部门的工作人员及有关人员对其内容负有保密责任。

第二章 授予专利权的条件

第二十二条 授予专利权的发明和实用新型，应当具备新颖性、创造性和实用性。

新颖性，是指该发明或者实用新型不属于现有技术；也没有任何单位或者个人就同样的发明或者实用新型在申请日以前向国务院专利行政部门提出过申请，并记载在申请日以后公布的专利申请文件或者公告的专利文件中。

创造性，是指与现有技术相比，该发明具有突出的实质性特点和显著的进步，该实用新型具有实质性特点和进步。

实用性，是指该发明或者实用新型能够制造或者使用，并且能够产生积极效果。

本法所称现有技术，是指申请日以前在国内外为公众所知的技术。

第二十三条 授予专利权的外观设计，应当不属于现有设计；也没有任何单位或者个人就同样的外观设计在申请日以前向国务院专利行政部门提出过申请，并记载在申请日以后公告的专利文件中。

授予专利权的外观设计与现有设计或者现有设计特征的组合相比，应当具有明显区别。

授予专利权的外观设计不得与他人在申请日以前已经取得的合法权利相冲突。

本法所称现有设计，是指申请日以前在国内外为公众所知的设计。

第二十四条 申请专利的发明创造在申请日以前六个月内，有下列情形之一的，不丧失新颖性：

（一）在国家出现紧急状态或者非常情况时，为公共利益目的首次公开的；

（二）在中国政府主办或者承认的国际展览会上首次展出的；

（三）在规定的学术会议或者技术会议上首次发表的；

（四）他人未经申请人同意而泄露其内容的。

第二十五条 对下列各项，不授予专利权：

（一）科学发现；

（二）智力活动的规则和方法；

（三）疾病的诊断和治疗方法；

（四）动物和植物品种；

（五）原子核变换方法以及用原子核变换方法获得的物质；

（六）对平面印刷品的图案、色彩或者二者的结合作出的主要起标识作用的设计。

对前款第（四）项所列产品的生产方法，可以依照本法规定授予专利权。

第三章　专利的申请

第二十六条　申请发明或者实用新型专利的，应当提交请求书、说明书及其摘要和权利要求书等文件。

请求书应当写明发明或者实用新型的名称，发明人的姓名，申请人姓名或者名称、地址，以及其他事项。

说明书应当对发明或者实用新型作出清楚、完整的说明，以所属技术领域的技术人员能够实现为准；必要的时候，应当有附图。摘要应当简要说明发明或者实用新型的技术要点。

权利要求书应当以说明书为依据，清楚、简要地限定要求专利保护的范围。

依赖遗传资源完成的发明创造，申请人应当在专利申请文件中说明该遗传资源的直接来源和原始来源；申请人无法说明原始来源的，应当陈述理由。

第二十七条　申请外观设计专利的，应当提交请求书、该外观设计的图片或者照片以及对该外观设计的简要说明等文件。

申请人提交的有关图片或者照片应当清楚地显示要求

专利保护的产品的外观设计。

第二十八条 国务院专利行政部门收到专利申请文件之日为申请日。如果申请文件是邮寄的，以寄出的邮戳日为申请日。

第二十九条 申请人自发明或者实用新型在外国第一次提出专利申请之日起十二个月内，或者自外观设计在外国第一次提出专利申请之日起六个月内，又在中国就相同主题提出专利申请的，依照该外国同中国签订的协议或者共同参加的国际条约，或者依照相互承认优先权的原则，可以享有优先权。

申请人自发明或者实用新型在中国第一次提出专利申请之日起十二个月内，或者自外观设计在中国第一次提出专利申请之日起六个月内，又向国务院专利行政部门就相同主题提出专利申请的，可以享有优先权。

第三十条 申请人要求发明、实用新型专利优先权的，应当在申请的时候提出书面声明，并且在第一次提出申请之日起十六个月内，提交第一次提出的专利申请文件的副本。

申请人要求外观设计专利优先权的，应当在申请的时候提出书面声明，并且在三个月内提交第一次提出的专利申请文件的副本。

申请人未提出书面声明或者逾期未提交专利申请文件副本的，视为未要求优先权。

第三十一条 一件发明或者实用新型专利申请应当限于一项发明或者实用新型。属于一个总的发明构思的两项以上的发明或者实用新型，可以作为一件申请提出。

一件外观设计专利申请应当限于一项外观设计。同一产品两项以上的相似外观设计，或者用于同一类别并且成套出售或者使用的产品的两项以上外观设计，可以作为一件申请提出。

第三十二条　申请人可以在被授予专利权之前随时撤回其专利申请。

第三十三条　申请人可以对其专利申请文件进行修改，但是，对发明和实用新型专利申请文件的修改不得超出原说明书和权利要求书记载的范围，对外观设计专利申请文件的修改不得超出原图片或者照片表示的范围。

第四章　专利申请的审查和批准

第三十四条　国务院专利行政部门收到发明专利申请后，经初步审查认为符合本法要求的，自申请日起满十八个月，即行公布。国务院专利行政部门可以根据申请人的请求早日公布其申请。

第三十五条　发明专利申请自申请日起三年内，国务院专利行政部门可以根据申请人随时提出的请求，对其申请进行实质审查；申请人无正当理由逾期不请求实质审查的，该申请即被视为撤回。

国务院专利行政部门认为必要的时候，可以自行对发明专利申请进行实质审查。

第三十六条　发明专利的申请人请求实质审查的时候，应当提交在申请日前与其发明有关的参考资料。

发明专利已经在外国提出过申请的，国务院专利行政部门可以要求申请人在指定期限内提交该国为审查其申请进行检索的资料或者审查结果的资料；无正当理由逾期不提交的，该申请即被视为撤回。

第三十七条　国务院专利行政部门对发明专利申请进行实质审查后，认为不符合本法规定的，应当通知申请人，要求其在指定的期限内陈述意见，或者对其申请进行修改；无正当理由逾期不答复的，该申请即被视为撤回。

第三十八条　发明专利申请经申请人陈述意见或者进行修改后，国务院专利行政部门仍然认为不符合本法规定的，应当予以驳回。

第三十九条　发明专利申请经实质审查没有发现驳回理由的，由国务院专利行政部门作出授予发明专利权的决定，发给发明专利证书，同时予以登记和公告。发明专利权自公告之日起生效。

第四十条　实用新型和外观设计专利申请经初步审查没有发现驳回理由的，由国务院专利行政部门作出授予实用新型专利权或者外观设计专利权的决定，发给相应的专利证书，同时予以登记和公告。实用新型专利权和外观设计专利权自公告之日起生效。

第四十一条　专利申请人对国务院专利行政部门驳回申请的决定不服的，可以自收到通知之日起三个月内向国务院专利行政部门请求复审。国务院专利行政部门复审后，作出决定，并通知专利申请人。

专利申请人对国务院专利行政部门的复审决定不服的，可以自收到通知之日起三个月内向人民法院起诉。

第五章　专利权的期限、终止和无效

第四十二条　发明专利权的期限为二十年，实用新型专利权的期限为十年，外观设计专利权的期限为十五年，均自申请日起计算。

自发明专利申请日起满四年，且自实质审查请求之日起满三年后授予发明专利权的，国务院专利行政部门应专利权人的请求，就发明专利在授权过程中的不合理延迟给予专利权期限补偿，但由申请人引起的不合理延迟除外。

为补偿新药上市审评审批占用的时间，对在中国获得上市许可的新药相关发明专利，国务院专利行政部门应专利权人的请求给予专利权期限补偿。补偿期限不超过五年，新药批准上市后总有效专利权期限不超过十四年。

第四十三条 专利权人应当自被授予专利权的当年开始缴纳年费。

第四十四条 有下列情形之一的，专利权在期限届满前终止：

（一）没有按照规定缴纳年费的；

（二）专利权人以书面声明放弃其专利权的。

专利权在期限届满前终止的，由国务院专利行政部门登记和公告。

第四十五条 自国务院专利行政部门公告授予专利权之日起，任何单位或者个人认为该专利权的授予不符合本法有关规定的，可以请求国务院专利行政部门宣告该专利权无效。

第四十六条 国务院专利行政部门对宣告专利权无效的请求应当及时审查和作出决定，并通知请求人和专利权人。宣告专利权无效的决定，由国务院专利行政部门登记和公告。

对国务院专利行政部门宣告专利权无效或者维持专利

权的决定不服的，可以自收到通知之日起三个月内向人民法院起诉。人民法院应当通知无效宣告请求程序的对方当事人作为第三人参加诉讼。

第四十七条　宣告无效的专利权视为自始即不存在。

宣告专利权无效的决定，对在宣告专利权无效前人民法院作出并已执行的专利侵权的判决、调解书，已经履行或者强制执行的专利侵权纠纷处理决定，以及已经履行的专利实施许可合同和专利权转让合同，不具有追溯力。但是因专利权人的恶意给他人造成的损失，应当给予赔偿。

依照前款规定不返还专利侵权赔偿金、专利使用费、专利权转让费，明显违反公平原则的，应当全部或者部分返还。

第六章　专利实施的特别许可

第四十八条　国务院专利行政部门、地方人民政府管理专利工作的部门应当会同同级相关部门采取措施，加强专利公共服务，促进专利实施和运用。

第四十九条　国有企业事业单位的发明专利，对国家利益或者公共利益具有重大意义的，国务院有关主管部门和省、自治区、直辖市人民政府报经国务院批准，可以决定在批准的范围内推广应用，允许指定的单位实施，由实施单位按照国家规定向专利权人支付使用费。

第五十条　专利权人自愿以书面方式向国务院专利行政部门声明愿意许可任何单位或者个人实施其专利，并明确许可使用费支付方式、标准的，由国务院专利行政部门予以公告，实行开放许可。就实用新型、外观设计专利提出开放许可声明的，应当提供专利权评价报告。

专利权人撤回开放许可声明的，应当以书面方式提出，并由国务院专利行政部门予以公告。开放许可声明被公告撤回的，不影响在先给予的开放许可的效力。

第五十一条　任何单位或者个人有意愿实施开放许可的专利的，以书面方式通知专利权人，并依照公告的许可使用费支付方式、标准支付许可使用费后，即获得专利实施许可。

开放许可实施期间，对专利权人缴纳专利年费相应给予减免。

实行开放许可的专利权人可以与被许可人就许可使用费进行协商后给予普通许可，但不得就该专利给予独占或者排他许可。

第五十二条　当事人就实施开放许可发生纠纷的，由当事人协商解决；不愿协商或者协商不成的，可以请求国务院专利行政部门进行调解，也可以向人民法院起诉。

第五十三条　有下列情形之一的，国务院专利行政部门根据具备实施条件的单位或者个人的申请，可以给予实施发明专利或者实用新型专利的强制许可：

（一）专利权人自专利权被授予之日起满三年，且自提出专利申请之日起满四年，无正当理由未实施或者未充分实施其专利的；

（二）专利权人行使专利权的行为被依法认定为垄断行为，为消除或者减少该行为对竞争产生的不利影响的。

第五十四条　在国家出现紧急状态或者非常情况时，或者为了公共利益的目的，国务院专利行政部门可以给予实施发明专利或者实用新型专利的强制许可。

第五十五条　为了公共健康目的，对取得专利权的药品，国务院专利行政部门可以给予制造并将其出口到符合中华人民共和国参加的有关国际条约规定的国家或者地区的强制许可。

第五十六条　一项取得专利权的发明或者实用新型比前已经取得专利权的发明或者实用新型具有显著经济意义的重大技术进步，其实施又有赖于前一发明或者实用新型的实施的，国务院专利行政部门根据后一专利权人的申请，可以给予实施前一发明或者实用新型的强制许可。

在依照前款规定给予实施强制许可的情形下，国务院专利行政部门根据前一专利权人的申请，也可以给予实施后一发明或者实用新型的强制许可。

第五十七条　强制许可涉及的发明创造为半导体技术的，其实施限于公共利益的目的和本法第五十三条第（二）项规定的情形。

第五十八条　除依照本法第五十三条第（二）项、第五十五条规定给予的强制许可外，强制许可的实施应当主要为了供应国内市场。

第五十九条　依照本法第五十三条第（一）项、第五十六条规定申请强制许可的单位或者个人应当提供证据，证明其以合理的条件请求专利权人许可其实施专利，但未能在合理的时间内获得许可。

第六十条　国务院专利行政部门作出的给予实施强制许可的决定，应当及时通知专利权人，并予以登记和公告。

给予实施强制许可的决定，应当根据强制许可的理由规定实施的范围和时间。强制许可的理由消除并不再发生时，国务院专利行政部门应当根据专利权人的请求，经审查后作出终止实施强制许可的决定。

第六十一条　取得实施强制许可的单位或者个人不享有独占的实施权，并且无权允许他人实施。

第六十二条　取得实施强制许可的单位或者个人应当付给专利权人合理的使用费，或者依照中华人民共和国参加的有关国际条约的规定处理使用费问题。付给使用费的，其数额由双方协商；双方不能达成协议的，由国务院专利行政部门裁决。

第六十三条　专利权人对国务院专利行政部门关于实施强制许可的决定不服的，专利权人和取得实施强制许可的单位或者个人对国务院专利行政部门关于实施强制许可的使用费的裁决不服的，可以自收到通知之日起三个月内向人民法院起诉。

第七章　专利权的保护

第六十四条　发明或者实用新型专利权的保护范围以其权利要求的内容为准，说明书及附图可以用于解释权利要求的内容。

外观设计专利权的保护范围以表示在图片或者照片中的该产品的外观设计为准，简要说明可以用于解释图片或者照片所表示的该产品的外观设计。

第六十五条　未经专利权人许可，实施其专利，即侵犯其专利权，引起纠纷的，由当事人协商解决；不愿协商或者协商不成的，专利权人或者利害关系人可以向人民法院起诉，也可以请求管理专利工作的部门处理。管理专利工作的部门处理时，认定侵权行为成立的，可以责令侵权人立即停止侵权行为，当事人不服的，可以自收到处理通知之日起十五日内依照《中华人民共和国行政诉讼法》向人民法院起诉；侵权人期满不起诉又不停止侵权行为的，管理专利工作的部门可以申请人民法院强制执行。进行处理的管理专利工作的部门应当事人的请求，可以就侵犯专利权的赔偿数额进行调解；调解不成的，当事人可以依照《中华人民共和国民事诉讼法》向人民法院起诉。

第六十六条　专利侵权纠纷涉及新产品制造方法的发明专利的，制造同样产品的单位或者个人应当提供其产品制造方法不同于专利方法的证明。

专利侵权纠纷涉及实用新型专利或者外观设计专利的，人民法院或者管理专利工作的部门可以要求专利权人或者利害关系人出具由国务院专利行政部门对相关实用新型或者外观设计进行检索、分析和评价后作出的专利权评价报告，作为审理、处理专利侵权纠纷的证据；专利权人、利害关系人或者被控侵权人也可以主动出具专利权评价报告。

第六十七条　在专利侵权纠纷中，被控侵权人有证据证明其实施的技术或者设计属于现有技术或者现有设计的，不构成侵犯专利权。

第六十八条　假冒专利的，除依法承担民事责任外，由负责专利执法的部门责令改正并予公告，没收违法所得，可以处违法所得五倍以下的罚款；没有违法所得或者违法所得在五万元以下的，可以处二十五万元以下的罚款；构成犯罪的，依法追究刑事责任。

第六十九条　负责专利执法的部门根据已经取得的证据，对涉嫌假冒专利行为进行查处时，有权采取下列措施：

（一）询问有关当事人，调查与涉嫌违法行为有关的情况；

（二）对当事人涉嫌违法行为的场所实施现场检查；

（三）查阅、复制与涉嫌违法行为有关的合同、发票、账簿以及其他有关资料；

（四）检查与涉嫌违法行为有关的产品；

（五）对有证据证明是假冒专利的产品，可以查封或者扣押。

管理专利工作的部门应专利权人或者利害关系人的请求处理专利侵权纠纷时，可以采取前款第（一）项、第（二）项、第（四）项所列措施。

负责专利执法的部门、管理专利工作的部门依法行使前两款规定的职权时，当事人应当予以协助、配合，不得拒绝、阻挠。

第七十条 国务院专利行政部门可以应专利权人或者利害关系人的请求处理在全国有重大影响的专利侵权纠纷。

地方人民政府管理专利工作的部门应专利权人或者利害关系人请求处理专利侵权纠纷，对在本行政区域内侵犯其同一专利权的案件可以合并处理；对跨区域侵犯其同一专利权的案件可以请求上级地方人民政府管理专利工作的部门处理。

第七十一条 侵犯专利权的赔偿数额按照权利人因被侵权所受到的实际损失或者侵权人因侵权所获得的利益确定；权利人的损失或者侵权人获得的利益难以确定的，参照该专利许可使用费的倍数合理确定。对故意侵犯专利权，情节严重的，可以在按照上述方法确定数额的一倍以上五倍以下确定赔偿数额。

权利人的损失、侵权人获得的利益和专利许可使用费均难以确定的，人民法院可以根据专利权的类型、侵权行为的性质和情节等因素，确定给予三万元以上五百万元以下的赔偿。

赔偿数额还应当包括权利人为制止侵权行为所支付的合理开支。

人民法院为确定赔偿数额，在权利人已经尽力举证，而与侵权行为相关的账簿、资料主要由侵权人掌握的情况下，可以责令侵权人提供与侵权行为相关的账簿、资料；侵权人不提供或者提供虚假的账簿、资料的，人民法院可以参考权利人的主张和提供的证据判定赔偿数额。

第七十二条 专利权人或者利害关系人有证据证明他人正在实施或者即将实施侵犯专利权、妨碍其实现权利的行为，如不及时制止将会使其合法权益受到难以弥补的损害的，可以在起诉前依法向人民法院申请采取财产保全、责令作出一定行为或者禁止作出一定行为的措施。

第七十三条 为了制止专利侵权行为，在证据可能灭失或者以后难以取得的情况下，专利权人或者利害关系人可以在起诉前依法向人民法院申请保全证据。

第七十四条 侵犯专利权的诉讼时效为三年，自专利权人或者利害关系人知道或者应当知道侵权行为以及侵权人之日起计算。

发明专利申请公布后至专利权授予前使用该发明未支付适当使用费的，专利权人要求支付使用费的诉讼时效为三年，自专利权人知道或者应当知道他人使用其发明之日起计算，但是，专利权人于专利权授予之日前即已知道或者应当知道的，自专利权授予之日起计算。

第七十五条 有下列情形之一的，不视为侵犯专利权：

（一）专利产品或者依照专利方法直接获得的产品，由专利权人或者经其许可的单位、个人售出后，使用、许诺销售、销售、进口该产品的；

（二）在专利申请日前已经制造相同产品、使用相同方法或者已经作好制造、使用的必要准备，并且仅在原有范围内继续制造、使用的；

（三）临时通过中国领陆、领水、领空的外国运输工具，依照其所属国同中国签订的协议或者共同参加的国际条约，或者依照互惠原则，为运输工具自身需要而在其装置和设备中使用有关专利的；

（四）专为科学研究和实验而使用有关专利的；

（五）为提供行政审批所需要的信息，制造、使用、进口专利药品或者专利医疗器械的，以及专门为其制造、进口专利药品或者专利医疗器械的。

第七十六条 药品上市审评审批过程中，药品上市许可申请人与有关专利权人或者利害关系人，因申请注册的药品相关的专利权产生纠纷的，相关当事人可以向人民法院起诉，请求就申请注册的药品相关技术方案是否落入他人药品专利权保护范围作出判决。国务院药品监督管理部门在规定的期限内，可以根据人民法院生效裁判作出是否暂停批准相关药品上市的决定。

药品上市许可申请人与有关专利权人或者利害关系人也可以就申请注册的药品相关的专利权纠纷，向国务院专利行政部门请求行政裁决。

国务院药品监督管理部门会同国务院专利行政部门制定药品上市许可审批与药品上市许可申请阶段专利权纠纷解决的具体衔接办法，报国务院同意后实施。

第七十七条　为生产经营目的使用、许诺销售或者销售不知道是未经专利权人许可而制造并售出的专利侵权产品，能证明该产品合法来源的，不承担赔偿责任。

第七十八条　违反本法第十九条规定向外国申请专利，泄露国家秘密的，由所在单位或者上级主管机关给予行政处分；构成犯罪的，依法追究刑事责任。

第七十九条　管理专利工作的部门不得参与向社会推荐专利产品等经营活动。

管理专利工作的部门违反前款规定的，由其上级机关或者监察机关责令改正，消除影响，有违法收入的予以没收；情节严重的，对直接负责的主管人员和其他直接责任人员依法给予处分。

第八十条　从事专利管理工作的国家机关工作人员以及其他有关国家机关工作人员玩忽职守、滥用职权、徇私舞弊，构成犯罪的，依法追究刑事责任；尚不构成犯罪的，依法给予处分。

第八章　附　　则

第八十一条　向国务院专利行政部门申请专利和办理其他手续，应当按照规定缴纳费用。

第八十二条　本法自 1985 年 4 月 1 日起施行。

Order of the President of the People's Republic of China

No. 55

The Decision of the Standing Committee of the National People's Congress on Amending the Patent Law of the People's Republic of China, adopted at the 22th Meeting of the Standing Committee of the Thirteenth National People's Congress on October 17, 2020, is hereby promulgated and shall go into effect on June 1, 2021.

Xi Jinping

President of the People's Republic of China

October 17, 2020

Patent Law of
the People's Republic of China

(Adopted at the 4th Meeting of the Standing Committee of the Sixth National People's Congress on March 12, 1984; amended for the first time in accordance with the Decision on Amending the Patent Law of the People's Republic of China at the 27th Meeting of the Standing Committee of the Seventh National People's Congress on September 4, 1992; amended for the second time in accordance with the Decision on Amending the Patent Law of the People's Republic of China at the 17th Meeting of the Standing Committee of the Ninth National People's Congress on August 25, 2000; amended for the third time in accordance with the Decision on Amending the Patent Law of the People's Republic of China at the 6th Meeting of the Standing Committee of the Eleventh National People's Congress on December 27, 2008; amended for the fourth time in accordance with the Decision on Amending the Patent Law of the People's Republic of China at the 22nd Meeting of the Standing Committee of the Thirteenth National People's Congress on October 17, 2020)

Contents

Chapter I
General Provisions

Article 1 This Law is enacted to protect the lawful rights and interests of patentees, to encourage invention-creation, to promote the exploitation of invention-creation, to enhance innovation capability, and to promote the advancement of science and technology and the development of economy and society.

Article 2 For the purposes of this Law, "invention-creations" mean inventions, utility models and designs.

"Invention" means any new technical solution proposed for a product, a process or the improvement thereof.

"Utility model" means any new technical solution proposed for the shape, the structure, or their combination, of a product, which is fit for practical use.

"Design" means, with respect to an overall or partial product, any new design of the shape, the pattern, or their combination, or the combination of the colour with shape or pattern, which is rich in an aesthetic appeal and is fit for industrial application.

Article 3 The patent administration department under the State Council shall be responsible for the administration of the patent-related work throughout the country. It shall accept and examine patent applications in a uniform way, and grant patent rights in accordance with law.

The departments in charge of patent affairs under the people's governments of provinces, autonomous regions and municipalities directly under the Central Government shall be responsible for the administrative work concerning patents within their respective administrative areas.

Article 4   Where an invention-creation for which a patent is applied for relates to national security or other major interests of the State and confidentiality needs to be maintained, the patent application shall be handled in accordance with the relevant prescriptions of the State.

Article 5   No patent right shall be granted for any invention-creation that violates laws or social morality or that is detrimental to the public interests.

No patent right shall be granted for any invention-creation where the acquisition or utilization of the genetic resources, on which the development of the invention-creation relies, violates the provisions of laws or administrative regulations.

Article 6   An invention-creation that is accomplished in the course of performing the duties of an employee, or mainly by using the material and technical conditions of an employer, is a service invention-creation. For a service invention-creation, the right to apply for a patent belongs to the employer. After such application is approved, the employer shall be the patentee. The employer may, in accordance with the law, dispose of the right to apply for a patent for its service invention-creation and the patent right, thereby facilitating the exploitation and utilization of the relevant invention-creation.

For a non-service invention-creation, the right to apply for a patent belongs to the inventor or designer. After the application is approved, the inventor or designer shall be the patentee.

For an invention-creation that is accomplished by using the material and technical conditions of an employer, if the employer has concluded a contract with the inventor or designer providing the ownership of the right to apply for the patent or the ownership of the patent right, such provision shall prevail.

Article 7 No entity or individual may prevent the inventor or designer from filing a patent application for a non-service invention-creation.

Article 8 For an invention-creation accomplished by two or more entities or individuals in collaboration, or accomplished by an entity or an invention-creation accomplished by an entity or individual in execution of a commission given to it or him by another entity or individual, the right to apply for a patent belongs, unless otherwise agreed upon, to the entity or individual that has accomplished the invention-creation, or to the entities or individuals that have accomplished the invention-creation in collaboration. After the application is approved, the entity(entities) or individual(s) that has(have) filed the application shall be the patentee(s).

Article 9 For any identical invention-creation, only one patent right shall be granted. However, where the same applicant files applications for both a utility model patent and an invention patent with regard to the identical invention-creation on the same day, if the utility model patent granted earlier has not been terminated and the applicant declares to abandon the utility model patent, the invention patent may be granted.

If two or more applicants file patent applications for the identical invention-creation respectively, the patent right shall be granted to the applicant whose application was filed first.

Article 10 The right to file a patent application and a patent right may be transferred.

Where a Chinese entity or individual transfers the right to file a patent application or a patent right to a foreigner, a foreign enterprise or any other foreign organization, the transfer shall go through the formalities in accordance with the relevant laws and administrative regulations.

Where the right to file a patent application or a patent right is transferred, the parties concerned shall enter into a written contract and register it with the patent administration department under the State Council. The patent administration department under the State Council shall make an announcement about the registration. The transfer of the right to file a patent application or the patent right shall take effect as of the date of registration.

Article 11　After the grant of the patent for an invention or an utility model, except where otherwise provided for in this Law, no entity or individual may, without the authorization of the patentee, exploit the patentee's patent, that is, for production or business purposes, manufacture, use, offer to sell, sell or import the patented product, or use the patented process, and use, offer to sell, sell or import the product directly obtained by the patented process.

After the grant of the patent for an design, no entity or individual may, without the authorization of the patentee, exploit the patentee's patent, that is, for production or business purposes, manufacture, offer to sell, sell or import the products incorporating the patentee's patented design.

Article 12　Any entity or individual exploiting the patent of another person shall enter into a license contract for exploitation with the patentee and pay the patentee a royalty for the exploitation of the patent. The licensee has no right to authorize any entity or individual, other than that referred to in the contract, to exploit the patent.

Article 13　After the publication of an invention patent application, the applicant may require the entity or individual exploiting the said invention to pay an appropriate amount of royalties.

Article 14　Where the co-owners of the right to file a patent application or of the patent right have reached an agreement on the exercise of the right, the agreement shall prevail. In the absence of such an agreement, any co-owner may independently exploit the patent or license another person to exploit the patent through a non-exclusive license; any royalty for the exploitation obtained from licensing others to exploit the patent shall be distributed among the co-owners.

Except for the circumstances as provided for in the preceding paragraph, the exercise of the co-owned right to file a patent application or the co-owned patent right shall be subject to the consent of all co-owners.

Article 15 The entity that is granted a patent right shall reward the inventor or designer of a service invention-creation. After such patent is exploited, the entity shall pay the inventor or designer a reasonable remuneration based on the extent of spreading and application as well as the economic benefits yielded.

The State encourages the entity that is granted a patent right to implement property right incentives, by such means as offering of stocks, options, and dividends, so that the inventor or designer can reasonably share the benefits of innovation.

Article 16 The inventor or designer shall have the right to be named as such in the patent documents.

The patentee shall have the right to have his patent indication displayed on the patented product or on the package of that product.

Article 17 Where any foreigner, foreign enterprise or other foreign organization without a habitual residence or business office in China files a patent application in China, the application shall be handled under this Law in accordance with the agreements concluded between the country to which the applicant belongs and China, or in accordance with the international treaties to which both the countries are parties, or in accordance with this Law on the basis of the principle of reciprocity.

Article 18 Where any foreigner, foreign enterprise or other foreign organization without a habitual residence or business office in China files a patent application or handles other patent-related matters in China, he or it shall entrust a legally established patent agency with the application or such matters.

Where any Chinese entity or individual files a patent application or handles other patent-related matters in China, he or it may entrust a legally established patent agency with the application or such matters.

The patent agency shall abide by laws and administrative regulations, and handle patent applications and other patent-related matters as entrusted by its principals. In respect of the contents of the principal's invention-creations, except for those that have been published or announced for patent application, the agency shall be obligated to keep them confidential. The specific measures for administration of the patent agencies shall be formulated by the State Council.

Article 19 Where any entity or individual intends to file a patent application abroad in a foreign country for any an invention or utility model accomplished in China, it or he shall submit the matter to request the patent administration department under the State Council for confidentiality examination in advance. The procedures and duration etc. of the confidentiality examination shall be carried out in accordance with the regulations of the State Council.

Any Chinese entity or individual may file for an international patent application in accordance with the relevant international treaties to which the People's Republic of China is a party. If an applicant files an international patent application, he or it shall abide by the provisions of the preceding paragraph.

The patent administration department under the State Council shall deal with international patent applications in accordance with the relevant international treaties to which the People's Republic of China is a party, this Law and the relevant regulations of the State Council.

For an invention or utility model, if a patent application has been filed in a foreign country in violation of the provisions of the first paragraph of this Article, it shall not be granted a patent right while filing a patent application in China.

Article 20　The principle of good faith shall be followed when filing a patent application and exercising patent rights. The patent rights may not be abused to harm the public interests or the lawful rights and interests of others.

For any misuse of patent rights for eliminating or restricting competition, if it constitutes a monopolistic conduct, it shall be dealt with in accordance with the Anti-Monopoly Law of the People's Republic of China.

Article 21　The patent administration department under the State Council shall deal with any patent application and patent-related request in accordance with the law and in conformity with the requirements of objectivity, fairness, accuracy and timeliness.

The patent administration department under the State Council shall strengthen the construction of a public service system for patent-related information, release patent-related information in a complete, accurate, and timely manner, provide basic data of patents, and publish patent gazettes on a regular basis, in order to promote dissemination and utilization of patent information.

Prior to the publication or announcement of a patent application, the staff members of the patent administration department under the State Council and the related personnel shall be obligated to keep its contents confidential.

Chapter II
Requirements for Granting Patent Rights

Article 22　Any invention or utility model for which a patent right is to be granted shall meet the requirements of novelty, inventiveness and practical use.

Novelty means that, the invention or utility model does not form part of the prior art; no entity or individual has filed a patent application for the identical invention or utility model with the patent administration department under the State Council before the filing date and the content of the application is disclosed in patent application documents published or patent documents announced after the filing date.

Inventiveness means that, as compared with the prior art, the invention has prominent substantive features and represents an obvious progress, and that the utility model has substantive features and represents a progress.

Practical use means that, the invention or utility model can be manufactured or used and can produce positive results.

For the purpose of this Law, "the prior art" refers to any technology known to the public domestically and/or abroad before the filing date.

Article 23　Any design for which a patent right is to be granted shall not be a prior design; no entity or individual has filed a patent application for the identical design with the patent administration department under the State Council before the filing date and the content of the application is disclosed in patent documents announced after the filing date.

Any design for which a patent right may be granted shall significantly differ from a prior design or the combination of prior design features.

Any design for which a patent right is granted must not conflict with the lawful rights acquired by any other person before the filing date.

For the purpose of this Law, "a prior design" refers to any design known to the public domestically and/or abroad before the filing date.

Article 24 Within six months before the filing date, an invention-creation for which a patent application is filed does not lose its novelty under any of the following circumstances:

(1) where it was made public for the first time for the purpose of the public interests when a state of emergency or an extraordinary situation occurred in the country;

(2) where it was exhibited for the first time at an international exhibition sponsored or recognized by the Chinese Government;

(3) where it was published for the first time at a prescribed academic or technological conference; or

(4) where its contents are divulged by another person without the consent of the applicant.

Article 25 No patent right shall be granted for any of the following:

(1) scientific discoveries;

(2) rules and methods for intellectual activities;

(3) methods for the diagnosis or treatment of diseases;

(4) animal and plant varieties;

(5) nuclear transformation methods and substances obtained by means of nuclear transformation;

(6) designs of two-dimensional printing goods, made of the pattern, the color or the combination of the two, which serve mainly as indicators.

The patent right may, in accordance with the provisions of this Law, be granted for the production methods of the products specified in Subparagraph (4) of the preceding paragraph.

Chapter III
Applications for Patents

Article 26 Where a patent application for an invention or utility model is filed, documents such as a request, a description and its abstract, and claims shall be submitted.

The request shall state the name of the invention or utility model, the name of the inventor, the name or title and the address of the applicant and other related matters.

The description shall contain a clear and comprehensive description of the invention or utility model so as to enable a person skilled in the relevant field of technology to carry it out; where necessary, drawings shall be attached to it. The abstract shall state briefly the main technical points of the invention or utility model.

The claims shall be based on the description and shall define the scope of the patent protection sought for in a clear and concise manner.

Where an invention-creation is accomplished by relying on genetic resources, the applicant shall indicate, in the patent application documents, the direct and original source of the genetic resources. Where the applicant fails to indicate the original source, he or it shall state the reasons thereof.

Article 27 Where a patent application for a design is filed, documents such as a request, drawings or photographs of the design and a brief description of the design shall be submitted.

The relevant drawings or photographs submitted by the applicant shall clearly indicate the design of the product for which patent protection is sought.

Article 28 The date on which the patent application documents are received by the patent administration department under the State Council shall be the filing date. If the application documents are delivered by post, the date of the postmark shall be the filing date.

Article 29 Where, within twelve months from the date on which any applicant first filed in a foreign country a patent application for an invention or utility model, or within six months from the date on which any applicant first filed in a foreign country a patent application for a design, he or it files in China a patent application for the same subject matter, he or it may enjoy the right of priority in accordance with the agreements concluded between the foreign country and China, or in accordance with the international treaties to which both countries are parties, or on the basis of the principle of mutual recognition of the right of priority.

Where, within twelve months from the date on which any applicant first filed in China a patent application for an invention or utility model, or within six months from the date on which any applicant first filed in China a patent application for a design, he or it files with the patent administration department under the State Council a patent application for the same subject matter, he or it may enjoy the right of priority.

Article 30 If any applicant claims the right of priority for an invention patent or a utility model patent, he or it shall make a written declaration when the patent application for an invention or utility model is filed, and submit, within sixteen months from the date on which the applicant first filed the application, a copy of the patent application documents which were filed for the first time.

If any applicant claims the right of priority for a design patent, he or it shall make a written declaration when the patent application for a design is filed, and submit, within three months, a copy of the patent application documents which were filed for the first time.

If the applicant fails to make the written declaration or to meet the time limit for submitting the copy of the patent application documents, the claim to the right of priority shall be deemed not to have been made.

Article 31   A patent application for an invention or utility model shall be limited to one invention or utility model. Two or more inventions or utility models belonging to a single general inventive concept may be filed as one application.

A patent application for a design shall be limited to one design. Two or more similar designs for the same product or two or more designs which are incorporated in products belonging to the same category and sold or used in sets may be filed as one application.

Article 32   An applicant may withdraw his or its patent application at any time before the patent right is granted.

Article 33   An applicant may amend his or its patent application documents, however, the amendment to the patent application documents for an invention or utility model may not go beyond the scope of disclosure contained in the original description and claims, and the amendment to the patent application documents for a design may not go beyond the scope of the disclosure as shown in the original drawings or photographs.

Chapter IV
Examination and Approval of
Patent Applications

Article 34   Where, after receiving a patent application for an invention, the patent administration department under the State Council finds that the application meets the requirements of this Law after preliminary examination, it shall publish the application promptly after the expiration of eighteen months from the filing date. Upon the request of the applicant, the patent administration department under the State Council may publish the application earlier.

Article 35 Within three years from the filing date, the patent administration department under the State Council may conduct a substantive examination of the application upon a request made by the applicant for a patent for invention at any time. If the applicant, without any justified reason, fails to request a substantive examination at the expiration of the time limit, the application shall be deemed to have been withdrawn.

When the patent administration department under the State Council deems it necessary, it may, on its own initiative, conduct a substantive examination of any patent application for an invention.

Article 36 When the applicant for an invention patent requests a substantive examination, he or it shall submit reference materials relating to the invention existing prior to the filing date.

If a patent application for an invention that has been filed in a foreign country, the patent administration department under the State Council may ask the applicant to submit, within a specified time limit, materials concerning any search made for the purpose of examining the application in that country, or concerning the results of any examination made in that country. If, at the expiration of the specified time limit, the said materials are not submitted without any justified reason, the application shall be deemed to have been withdrawn.

Article 37 After the patent administration department under the State Council has conducted a substantive examination of the patent application for an invention, if it finds that the application is not in conformity with the provisions of this Law, it shall notify the applicant and require him or it to state opinions within a specified time limit or to amend the application. If the applicant fails to state opinions at the expiration of the specified time limit without any justified reason, the application shall be deemed to have been withdrawn.

Article 38　After the applicant states his or its opinions on or makes amendment to the patent application for an invention, the patent administration department under the State Council still finds that the patent application for an invention is not in conformity with the provisions of this Law, the application shall be rejected.

Article 39　Where no cause for rejection is found after the substantive examination of the patent application for an invention, the patent administration department under the State Council shall make a decision to grant the patent right for invention, issue the certificate of patent for invention, and meanwhile make a registration and announcement about it. The patent right for invention shall take effect as of the date of the announcement.

Article 40　Where no cause for rejection is found after the preliminary examination of the patent application for a utility model or design, the patent administration department under the State Council shall make a decision to grant the patent right for utility model or design, issue a corresponding patent certificate, and meanwhile make a registration and announcement about it. The patent right for utility model or design shall take effect as of the date of the announcement.

Article 41　Where a patent applicant refuses to accept the decision of the patent administration department under the State Council on rejecting the application, the applicant may, within three months from the date of receipt of the notification, request the patent administration department under the State Council to make a reexamination. The patent administration department under the State Council shall, after reexamination, make a decision and notify the patent applicant.

Where the patent applicant refuses to accept the decision of the reexamination of the patent administration department under the State Council, it or he may, within three months from the date of receipt of the notification, file a lawsuit in the people's court.

Chapter V
Terms, Termination and
Invalidation of Patent Rights

Article 42   The term of patent right for inventions shall be twenty years, the term of patent right for utility models shall be ten years, and the term of patent right for designs shall be fifteen years, all commencing from the filing date.

Where a patent right for an invention is granted after the expiration of four years from the filing date and after the expiration of three years from the date of the request for substantive examination of the application, the patent administration department under the State Council shall, at the request of the patentee, extend the term of the patent to compensate for the unreasonable delay in the granting process of the invention, except for the unreasonable delay caused by the applicant.

In order to compensate for the time taken for the review and approval process before the marketing of a new pharmaceutical product, the patent administration department under the State Council shall, at the request of the patentee, extend the term of the new pharmaceutical-related invention which has been approved for marketing in China. The compensation term may not be more than five years, and the total effective term of the patent right may not be more than fourteen years from the date of marketing approval.

Article 43 The patentee shall pay an annual fees beginning with the year in which the patent right is granted.

Article 44 Under any of the following circumstances, the patent right shall be terminated before the expiration of its term:

(1) failure to pay the annual fee as required; or

(2) the patentee waiving of the patent right by a written declaration.

If a patent right terminated before the term expires, the patent administration department under the State Council shall register and announce such termination.

Article 45 Beginning from the date of the announcement of the grant of a patent right by the patent administration department under the State Council, any entity or individual considers that the grant of the patent right is not in conformity with the relevant provisions of this Law, it or he may request the patent administration department under the State Council to declare the patent right invalid.

Article 46 The patent administration department under the State Council shall, in a timely manner, examine the request for declaring invalidation of a patent right invalid, make a decision on it, and notify the person who made the request and the patentee of its decision. The decision on declaring the patent right invalid shall be registered and announced by the patent administration department under the State Council.

Where the party concerned refuses to accept the decision of the patent administration department under the State Council on declaring the patent right invalid or on upholding the patent right, he or it may file a lawsuit in the people's court within three months from the date of receipt of the notification of the decision. The people's court shall notify the person who is the opponent party in the invalidation procedure to participate in the litigation as a third party.

Article 47   Any patent right that has been declared invalid is deemed to be non-existent from the beginning.

The decision on declaring the patent right invalid shall have no retroactive effect on any judgment or mediation statement on patent infringement which has been made and enforced by the people's court, on any decision concerning the handling of a dispute over patent infringement which has been performed or compulsorily executed, or on any patent exploitation licensing contract or patent right transfer contract which has been performed – prior to the declaration of the invalidation of the patent right; however, the damage caused to other persons in bad faith by the patentee shall be compensated.

Where the monetary damage for patent infringement, the royalties for patent exploitation or the fees for the transfer of the patent right is not refunded pursuant to the provisions of the preceding paragraph, but such non-refund is obviously contrary to the principle of fairness, refund shall be made fully or partly.

Chapter VI
Special License for the Exploitation of a Patent

Article 48   The patent administration department under the State Council and the departments in charge of patent affairs of the local people's government shall, in conjunction with the relevant departments at the same level, take measures to strengthen patent public services and promote the exploitation and utilization of patents.

Article 49   Where any patent for invention of a State-owned enterprise or institution, is of great significance to the interest of the State or to the public interests, the relevant competent departments under the State Council and the people's governments of provinces, autonomous regions or municipalities directly under the Central Government may, after approval by the State Council, decide that the patented invention be spread and applied within the approved scope, and allow designated entities to exploit the invention. The exploiting entity shall, in accordance with the regulations of the State, pay a royalty to the patentee.

Article 50   Where the patentee voluntarily declares in writing to the patent administration department under the State Council that it or he is willing to license any entity or individual to exploit its or his patent, and specifies the payment method and the standard of the royalty, the patent administration department under the State Council shall make an announcement and implement an open license. Where the patentee submits an open license statement for its or his utility model and design, it or he shall attach an evaluation report of the patent.

Where the patentee withdraws the open license statement, the withdrawal shall be submitted in writing and be announced by the patent administration department under the State Council. If the open license statement is withdrawn by announcement, the validity of the open license granted earlier shall not be affected.

Article 51   Where an entity or individual notifies the patentee of its or his willing to implement an open-licensed patent in writing and pays the royalty in accordance with the announced payment method and standard for the royalty, it or he obtains the patent license.

During the implementation period of the open license, the annual fee paid by the patentee shall be reduced or exempted accordingly.

The patentee whose patent is under an open license may grant a general license after negotiating with the licensee on the royalty, however, the patentee may not grant an exclusive or sole license for that patent.

Article 52   Where a dispute arises over the implementation of an open license, the parties shall resolve it through consultation. Where the parties are unwilling to consult with each other or where the consultation fails, they may either request the patent administration department under the State Council to mediate the matter, or file a lawsuit in the people's court.

Article 53   Under any of the following circumstances, the patent administration department under the State Council may, upon the application made by an entity or individual which possesses the conditions for exploitation, grant a compulsory license to exploit an invention or utility model:

(1) where the patentee, after the expiration of three years from the date of the grant of the patent right and the expiration of four years from the filing date, has not exploited or has not sufficiently exploited the patent without any justified reason; or

(2) where the exercise of the patent right by the patentee is confirmed as a monopolistic conduct in accordance with law, and its negative impact on competition needs to be eliminated or reduced.

Article 54   Where a national emergency or any extraordinary state of affairs occurs, or where the public interests so require, the patent administration department under the State Council may grant a compulsory license to exploit the patent for invention or utility model.

Article 55   For the purposes of public health, the patent administration department under the State Council may grant a compulsory license for manufacture of a pharmaceutical product, for which a patent right has been granted, and for exporting it to the countries or regions that comply with the provisions of the relevant international treaties to which the People's Republic of China is a party.

Article 56   Where the invention or utility model, for which a patent right has been granted, involves a major technological advancement of remarkable economic significance, compared with an invention or utility model for which a patent right has been granted earlier, and the exploitation of the later invention or utility model depends on the exploitation of the earlier invention or utility model, the patent administration department under the State Council may, upon the request of the patentee of the later patent, grant a compulsory license to exploit the earlier invention or utility model.

In the case of granting a compulsory license in accordance with the provisions of the preceding paragraph, the patent administration department under the State Council may, upon the request of the patentee of the earlier patent, also grant a compulsory license to exploit the later invention or utility model.

Article 57   Where the invention-creation involved in a compulsory license is a semi-conductor technology, the exploitation thereof shall be limited to the purpose of the public interests and to the circumstances as provided for in Subparagraph (2) of Article 53 of this Law.

Article 58   Except for the compulsory licenses granted in accordance with the provisions of Subparagraph (2) of Article 53 or Article 55 of this Law, compulsory licenses shall mainly be exercised for the supply to the domestic market.

Article 59　Any entity or individual applying for a compulsory license in accordance with the provisions of Subparagraph (1) of Article 53 or Article 56 of this Law shall provide evidence to prove that it or he has made a request for a license from the patentee to exploit the patent under reasonable terms, but has failed to obtain such a license within a reasonable period of time.

Article 60　The decision made by the patent administration department under the State Council on granting a compulsory license for exploitation shall be notified to the patentee in a timely manner and shall be registered and announced.

In the decision on granting the compulsory license for exploitation, the scope and duration of the exploitation shall be specified on the basis of the reasons justifying the grant. When the circumstances which led to such compulsory license cease to exist and no longer occur, the patent administration department under the State Council shall, at the request of the patentee, make a decision to terminate the compulsory license after examination.

Article 61　Any entity or individual that is granted a compulsory license for exploitation does not have an exclusive right to exploit, nor has it or he the right to allow others to exploit.

Article 62　The entity or individual that is granted a compulsory license for exploitation shall pay reasonable royalties to the patentee, or deal with the issue of royalties in accordance with the provisions of the relevant international treaties to which the People's Republic of China is a party. Where royalties are paid, the amount of royalties shall be negotiated by both parties. Where the parties fail to reach an agreement, the patent administration department under the State Council shall make a ruling.

Article 63 Where the patentee refuses to accept the decision of the patent administration department under the State Council on granting a compulsory license for exploitation, or where the patentee and the entity or individual that is granted the compulsory license for exploitation refuses to accept the ruling made by the patent administration department under the State Council regarding the royalties for the compulsory license for exploitation, it or he may, within three months from the date of receipt of the notification, file a lawsuit in the people's court.

Chapter VII
Protection of Patent Rights

Article 64 For the patent right of an invention or a utility model, the scope of protection shall be confined to the content of the claims. The description and the drawings attached may be used to explain the content of the claims.

For the patent right for design, the scope of protection shall be confined to the design of the product as shown in the drawings or photographs. The brief description may be used to explain the design of the product as shown in the drawings or photographs.

Article 65 Where a dispute arises as a result of the exploitation of a patent without the authorization of the patentee, that is, the infringement of the patentee's patent right, it shall be resolved through consultation between the parties. Where the parties are unwilling to consult with each other or where the consultation fails, the patentee or any interested party may file a lawsuit in the people's court, or request the departments in charge of patent-related work to deal with the dispute. When the department in charge of patent-related work dealing with the dispute considers that the infringement is established, it may order the infringer to stop the infringing act immediately. If the infringer refuses to accept the order, he may, within fifteen days from the date of receipt of the notification of the order, file a lawsuit in the people's court in accordance with the Administrative Procedure Law of the People's Republic of China. If the infringer neither files a lawsuit nor stops the infringing act at the expiration of the period of time, the department in charge of patent-related work may file an application with the people's court for compulsory execution. At the request of the party concerned, the department in charge of patent-related work dealing with the dispute may carry out mediation concerning the amount of compensation for the patent right infringement. If the mediation fails, the parties may file a lawsuit in the people's court in accordance with the Civil Procedure Law of the People's Republic of China.

Article 66　Where a patent infringement dispute involves a patent for an invention for a manufacturing process of a new product, the entity or individual manufacturing the identical product shall provide evidence to prove that the manufacturing process used in the manufacture of its or his product is different from the patented process.

Where a patent infringement dispute involves a patent for a utility model or a design, the people's court or the department in charge of patent-related work may ask the patentee or any interested party to furnish a patent right evaluation report made by the patent administration department under the State Council after having conducted search, analysis and evaluation of the relevant utility model or design, and use it as evidence for hearing or dealing with the patent infringement dispute; the patentee or any interested party or the alleged infringer may also voluntarily furnish the patent right evaluation report.

Article 67　In a patent infringement dispute, if the alleged infringer has evidence to prove that the technology or design exploited by it or him forms part of the prior art or prior design, such exploitation shall not constitute an infringement of the patent right.

Article 68   Where any person counterfeits a patent of another person, he shall, in addition to bearing his civil liabilities in accordance with law, be ordered by the department in charge of patent enforcement to make rectifications, and the department shall make the matter known to the public. His illegal earnings shall be confiscated and, in addition, he may be imposed on a fine of not more than five times his illegal earnings. If there are no illegal earnings or the illegal earnings are less than RMB 50,000 yuan, a fine of not more than RMB 250,000 yuan may be imposed on him. Where the infringement constitutes a crime, he shall be investigated for his criminal responsibility in accordance with law.

Article 69   When investigating and handling the suspected act of counterfeiting a patent, the department in charge of patent enforcement shall have the right to take the following measures based on the evidence obtained:

(1) to inquire the parties concerned, and investigate the circumstances related to the suspected illegal act;

(2) to carry out an on-the-spot inspection of the site where the party's suspected illegal act is committed;

(3) to consult and duplicate the contracts, invoices, account books and other relevant materials related to the suspected illegal act;

(4) to examine the products related to the suspected illegal act;

(5) to seal up or detain the products proved to be produced by the counterfeited patent.

When dealing with the patent infringement disputes at the request of the patentee or the interested party, the department in charge of patent-related work may take measures listed in Subparagraph (1),(2) and (4) of the preceding paragraph.

When the department in charge of patent enforcement or the department in charge of patent-related work exercises its functions and powers as stipulated in the preceding two paragraphs in accordance with law, the parties concerned shall provide assistance and cooperation and shall not refuse to do so or create obstacles.

Article 70　The patent administration department under the State Council may, at the request of the patentee or any interested party, deal with patent infringement disputes that have a major impact throughout the country.

When dealing with patent infringement disputes at the request of the patentee or any interested party, the department in charge of patent-related work of the local people's government may deal with the cases of infringement of the same patent right within its administrative area in a combined manner; for cases infringing the same patent right across administrative areas, it may request the department in charge of patent-related work of the local people's government at a higher level to deal with the matter.

Article 71　The amount of compensation for patent right infringement shall be determined on the basis of the actual losses suffered by the right holder as a result of the infringement or the profits earned by the infringer as a result of the infringement. Where it is difficult to determine the losses suffered by the right holder or the profits earned by the infringer, the amount shall be reasonably determined by reference to the multiple of the amount of the royalties for the patent license. For intentional infringement of a patent right, if the circumstances are serious, the amount of compensation may be determined at not less than one time and not more than five times the amount determined in accordance with the above-mentioned method.

Where it is difficult to determine the losses suffered by the right holder, the profits earned by the infringer and the royalties for the patent license, the people's court may determine the amount of compensation, which is not less than RMB 30,000 yuan and not more than RMB 5,000,000 yuan, in light of such factors as the type of the patent right, the nature and the circumstances of the infringing act.

The amount of compensation shall also include the reasonable expenses of the right holder paid for putting an end to the infringement.

In order to determine the amount of compensation, under the circumstance that the right holder has tried its or his best to provide evidence, and the account books or materials related to the patent infringement are mainly at the hands of the infringer, the people's court may order the infringer to provide such account books or materials. Where the infringer refuses to provide the account books or materials, or provides false account books or materials, the people's court may determine the amount of compensation by reference to the right holder's claims and the evidence provided.

Article 72 Where the patentee or any interested party has evidence to prove that another person is infringing or is about to infringe its or his patent right or hinders the realization of the right, which, unless being stopped in time, may cause irreparable damage to his lawful rights and interests, it or he may, before filing a lawsuit, apply to the people's court for adopting measures for property preservation, ordering to do certain acts or to prohibit certain acts in accordance with the law.

Article 73 In order to stop patent infringement, in cases where the evidence might be destroyed or where it would be difficult to obtain in the future, the patentee or the interested party may, before filing a lawsuit, apply to the people's court for evidence preservation in accordance with the law.

Article 74   The period of limitation for action against the infringement of a patent right is three years, beginning from the date on which the patentee or interested party knows or should have known of the infringing act and the infringer.

Where an appropriate royalty is not paid for exploiting an invention during the period from the publication of the application to the grant of the patent right, the limitation period for taking legal action by the patentee for requesting the payment of royalties is three years, beginning from the date on which the patentee knows or should have known of the exploitation of his or its invention by another person. However, where the patentee knows or should have known of the exploitation of the invention before the patent right is granted, the period of limitation for action shall begin from the date when the patent right is granted.

Article 75   None of the following shall be deemed as infringement of the patent right:

(1) where, after the sale of a patented product or a product acquired directly in accordance with a patented process by the patentee or any entity or individual authorized by the patentee, any other person uses, offers to sell, sells, or imports that product;

(2) where, before the filing date of the patent application, any person who has already manufactured the identical product, used the identical process, or made necessary preparations for its manufacturing or using, continues to manufacture or use it only within the original scope;

(3) where any foreign means of transport, which temporarily passes through the territory, territorial waters or territorial airspace of China, uses the relevant patent in its devices or installations for its own needs in accordance with the agreements concluded between the country to which the foreign means of transport belongs and China, or in accordance with the international treaties to which both countries are parties, or on the basis of the principle of reciprocity;

(4) where the relevant patent is used specially for the purposes of scientific research and experimentation; or

(5) where for the purposes of providing information needed for the administrative examination and approval, any person manufactures, uses, or imports patented drugs or patented medical apparatus and instruments, or any other person manufactures or imports patented drugs or patented medical apparatus and instruments especially for that person.

Article 76　In the review and approval process before the marketing of a pharmaceutical product, where the applicant for marketing approval of the pharmaceutical product has any disputes over the relevant patent right associated with the pharmaceutical product applied for registration with the relevant patentee or interested party, the party concerned may file a lawsuit before the people's court and request a judgment on whether the technical solution related to the pharmaceutical product that is applied for registration falls within the protection scope of any pharmaceutical product patent right owned by others. The medical product regulatory department under the State Council may, within a prescribed time limit, make a decision on whether to suspend the marketing approval of the pharmaceutical product according to the effective judgment or written order of the people's court.

The applicant for marketing approval of the pharmaceutical product, the relevant patentee or the interested party may also petition the patent administration department under the State Council for an administrative adjudication on the disputes over the patent right associated with the drug applied for registration.

The medical products regulatory department under the State Council shall, in conjunction with the patent administration department under the State Council, formulate specific cohesive measures for patent right dispute resolutions at the stages of pharmaceutical product marketing license approval and pharmaceutical product marketing license application, which shall be implemented after the approval of the State Council.

Article 77　Any person who, for production and business purposes, uses, offers to sell or sells a patent-infringing product, without knowing that it is manufactured and sold without the authorization of the patentee, may not be liable for compensation provided that he can prove the legitimate source of the product.

Article 78　Where any person, in violation of the provisions of Article 19 of this Law, files a patent application in a foreign country, thereby divulging a State secret, the entity to which he belongs or the competent authority at the higher level shall impose on him an administrative sanction; if a crime is established, he shall be investigated for his criminal responsibility in accordance with the law.

Article 79　The departments in charge of patent-related work under the people's governments may not take part in recommending any patented product for sale to the public or any such commercial activities.

Where a department in charge of patent-related work under the people's governments violates the provisions of the preceding paragraph, it shall be ordered to make a rectification and to eliminate adverse effects by the department at the higher level or the supervisory organ. The illegal earnings, if any, shall be confiscated. Where the circumstances are serious, the principal leading person directly in charge and other persons who are directly responsible shall be given sanctions in accordance with the law.

Article 80　Where a State functionary working for patent administration or any other State functionary concerned neglects his duties, abuses his powers, or engages in malpractice for personal gain, which constitutes a crime, shall be investigated for his criminal responsibility in accordance with the law. If the case is not serious enough to constitute a crime, he shall be given sanctions in accordance with the law.

Chapter VIII
Supplementary Provisions

Article 81   To file a patent application or go through other formalities with the patent administrative department under the State Council, fees shall be paid as prescribed.

Article 82   This Law shall go into effect on 1 April, 1985.